5·20·77

Eyes on the Street

Eyes on the Street
David Rosenthal

Barlenmir House

Barlenmir House, Publishers, New York, N.Y.

ISBN: 0-87929-032-3
Library of Congress Catalog Card Number: 73-92350
First Edition
Printed in the United States of America
Book & Cover Design by Steffan

Poems in this volume appear in the following pub-
lications to which acknowledgement and thanks are
made: *The Humanist, Open Places, The Nation, The
New York Times, Perstare, Poetry* (Chicago), and
The Quarterly Review of Literature.

For my father and mother

1961270

PART ONE

Frost

The white, wrinkled day howls.
I look out my window.
The green-yellow of life is gone.
Nature marks her victims with chalk.

Vicious Dog

Vicious dog,
you squint from behind
a high lacy fence
on Hudson Street,
and the moon is a pale bowl
of exhaustion.
Your eyes glint
with a wan listless
albumen.
What is meant by your
muscular
angry pose?
You yawn in the heat.
(In the liquid night
someone is playing Bach on a trumpet.)
Hysterical at two cops
passing your square domain,
you are a million years
too late.

Overbrook Sanitarium

To James Moody

"Where the moving dead still talk." —Anne Sexton

At the station, Doctor Paitch,
the night wet my soles.
Staring with the large eyes of a bee,
watching houses without windows
(all their lights were off),
clinging to my white-hot pole, I saw you pick
your way through a sea of air
to say that I was there. You took my things.
Over station walls, the trees drooped tired boughs.
August had made them squirm in the rosy heat.
Doctor Paitch, you came with soft feet,
unclenching my hands from milkweed.
With large eyes I saw you moving
in the silent station:
dead end.

Remembering Dilys Laing

Dilys,
I am watching a flower through a cloud of pink smoke,
frightening birds from the rock,
watching a crow upon rippling air.

You have roots in your hair now.
They embrace,
like a small, white boy wrapped round a tree,
his white hands,
his white nails digging into the bark.
                    And I am standing watching,
                    wanting to touch him and afraid.
                    He is so still.

                    I sat beneath the roof of trees
                    crying,
                    amplified by death,
                    and a night
                    orange spotted.

There is a cemetery where
fog spirals a million flowers
through yesterday's rain
                    but
there is one flower that shocks
like the hideous hand of a frog.
Its moist tenderness is bruised by fingers.

I am watching the flower,
through a cloud of pink smoke,
watching a crow upon rippling air.

To William Carlos Williams: Promontory Point

I think you are so very lucky.

Walk down this sullen Negro street,
to where the street, suddenly,
                              runs
                                    into
the bright chalky blaze of water and sky,
climbs, glorying,
up out of the icy, despairing city.

And the wispy indifferent sighs of seagulls
crackle down upon the rooftops of 61st Street,
today.

Run down to the tip of the water.
The gulls spin through the pink sky
on noiseless indifferent wings.

He was the man who got inside
the contorted harrowing face of weeping:
the tortured, misshapen mouth;
the eyebrows, clinched together;
the shining eyelashes, shut tight.

Run down to the tip of the water.
See the new day frolic and chuckle
upon the shiny newborn ribbons of beach, of
        water, of sky.
Twist your feet in the cracked sand,
roll your body in the warmth,
and lie still, listen,
watch the giddy joke
of water and sky.

I think you are very lucky.

New Year

It must be because of you that I see now
how the sun runs riot
                runs riot
today,
in our room.
How I want to touch the spot
where shadow becomes white skin on your neck:
a damp fusion of colors.

And I see how the caressing air moves
like the sound of purring,
rubbing in waves up against the four flesh-colored walls.

Today your shiny hair flows
an unconscious disarray
across the pillow.
How small and curled you are this morning
with your lips pursed,
your eyes shut tight
in a tight, puzzled question-mark.

I see how this lacelight
flows in icy ripples,
in circles round the room.

It must be because of you that today is a day for free
that I am glad to roll around in,
to watch my words fade backwards:
diminishing ribbons of sound,
and the plastic rose in the beer bottle swoon upwards,
upside down.

There are places on your neck your shoulders and
your arms where the smiling petals of skin fold
gently outward.
I will touch you there, all the soft yielding things
about you, everyday everyday. It is a
new year.

Neapolitan Pleasure Cruise

The breeze seems to engulf you
in sighs of weary delight.
O Mister how I rejoice to watch
the way your red-striped blazer flaps
against your legs.
The way your chocolate mustaches go
wiggle-wiggle.
The wind blows candy kisses
from your eyes to mine
and back.
We ride the pleasure boat together.

From the beach the boat
is a smeared dead insect. Overhead
two helicopters cough, rattle, gape.
And the dark boys on the beach squirm.
Two,
        nothing but pain
                        in their heads
flick back their hair
and grin.

They run barefoot across the sand
to the cave at the back of the beach.
The cold there makes them sneeze.

Pull down your pants.

When I went below
to buy Juju fruits at the candy counter
I saw you follow me, squinting.

On the deck,
the clouds melt and fold
overhead.
How I can sink my twitching thumbs and fingers
into your marshmallow face.
But you are already crumpling
like a piece of burning paper.
I hear one lady shriek as the water
furrows and seethes in the wind.
While you crumple with your heart pounding
against the overcast deck,
I pretend
it is the end
of the world.

This It Is

You say
the yellow light — is on.
I say
I don't see it.
I see the window
fill up with grey smoky sunlight.
Red pigeons' eyes look in at me,
knowing nothing, nothing knowing,
not seeing.

You sit at the table
laughing, then not.
My self drains out of me,
my body turns pale white,
while a moth rustles briefly,
then escapes above the buildings
where dirty children dart along
the edges of black roofs.
The wings beat and burn noiselessly
inside my head.

In the hallway,
crowded by feet and garbage,
my paper heart is burning,
turning from side to side
like a troubled sleeper.

Dead Baby, Sleep in Heavenly Bliss

For N. and our unborn child

The color returns. I see
spring.
The trees spray their pale green confetti
all over.
On the road to the airport
we sit in the back seat
not looking, not talking.
I dream the wrinkled little face,
ancient and intense,
the dry mouth
howling, banging in the still air,
howling incessantly,
the little clenched fists.
The dotted red death-lines
spread rapidly
before
before my eyes.
They squirm
with wild energy
across the scalp.
A dry cough explodes in the still air.

The tiny buds reveal
their small secrets
to the breeze.
It is like cool hands
brushing through the depths of foliage.

These new beginnings, again.
And by the side of the road,
maidens dance through the steamy heat.
They dance disconsolately,
with dark eyes, waltzing
through the passionate deeps
of forgetfulness.

After Four Years, Back on Hampstead Heath Again

My eyes
fill
with these new stars,
floating in the
                    upward boughs,
the deep green
where the crows,
only too luxurious, silky,
flap in the twilight.

                    A narrowing tunnel
                    dense with darkness
                    O how I
                    long to fling myself
                    into the wet undergrowth
                    and lie still.

Withdrawal

Can you endure a night
of endless torture,
of torture neverending?

— mother, moaning and sweating
at the bedside,
gently
        from side
                to side,
in the blackest blacks of early morning.

I look up
as the air shifts
and diminishes
all our objects,
look up
from the bottom of a deep, deep pool,
look up
at the surface, creased and turgid
with movement never ending,
all our objections
and proposals
are held tight at the breast.

On my ceiling
I envision
a swirling mass of eyeballs
all shapes
all sizes
all glaring brutally downward
with the look of doom in them.

We sit,
moaning, swaying gently,
bodies barely touching,
together in the last agonies
the last
and most fervid agonies
the gentle hand that rocked me
all year long
withdrawing steadily
ever more distant withdrawal
till I can only lie
panting, flat on my back,
clutching a fading staircase of light
that mounts the wall.

Oh mother I am sick
sick to death
will you turn your head
toward me
your eyes
are twin beacons of fear
falling thick
thick as leaves.
All around me,
the blackened charred stumps
of last month's gentle raptures
of heavenly indrawn bliss.

"The Lord giveth and
        the Lord taketh
away.
Blessed be the name of the Lord."

What is this endless staircase:
objections, arguments,
impediments,
where yesterday I beheld
only myself in a perfect mirror,
a gracious plaything to be held
in the palm of the hand.

Oh mother! I am being dragged out
into the agonies — the chills and
hot thrills of this world.

I recognize another form
by the side of the bed,
swaying reluctantly against mine.
You sit
watching me
give birth to myself
in the ice-cold raptures
of early morning.

Time moves so slowly
I could swear
it fidgeted backwards
just then.
Its flow is irregular
irregular at best
yet it holds the seminal sources
of our closest contact,
blood draining away from the hands
as they close in a desperate grip.

By the side of the bed you watch.
We draw closer together.
The light rises.

The room becomes light.
I lie,
spent and shaking
on the bed.
By the side of the bed you watch.

Saudade do Heroin

Autumn 1965

"You going to need lots of dope
with the winter coming."
So say Archie
and right away the wind
blows a coughing dry river of leaves
round the old house, Perry Street
and we sit hunched over in the fog
getting off in the halflit living room.
The record coughs,
an old, old tune, spick music.
On the label a lady inclines
curlicues of art nouveau.
It is like Dr. Meltzer's Soothing Syrup,
the dope of another era.
Was it the same sweet metallic blow
somewhere towards the back of the head?
I can neither believe nor imagine.

I walk home from the bus,
two bags of doo-gee in my wallet,
and I am wrapped in the cold winds of childhood.
Two-family houses and neighborhood stores
pipe the nostalgic music through my veins.
It is autumn, eastern America,
and the bitter stinging wind
kisses the treetops,
where brown crumpled leaves still cluster.
The breathing and breathless voice-whispers
of children,
the smell of leaves
burning in piles in the street
where young voices and bicycles move,
breathless in evening.
All this is syrup — sweet, sweet syrup,
withdrawal-intensity of nostalgia
pulsing at the back of the head.

All this loving, this fine mellow loving
drains through me. I mount the steps
and am inside.

The sweet limp syrup,
twice craved,
drains out of the dropper.
Sit back.
First. . . . the sweet blow in the viscera.
Then, it is like the clean metallic vapor
of hospitals,
the muskiness of unwashed genitals,
all the scents
of the holy man.
Slightly out of breath, warm,
the familiar presence beating
like hot wings inside my head,
I drop back in the chair.
The dropper is empty.

At dusk,
the wind rattles magic bones outside the window,
in a strange and lovely foreign tongue.

Chicago: the Mac Man

To Archie Shepp

On the south side,
the spade children play in circles in the empty streets.
Flushed and breathless in October, they run
through the thin, restless air of boyish dreams,
and blow cupid's bubbles round and round.

It is indeed violent.
We have been told. There is need of the cutting arm
under the streetlamp, of the
fist swinging in circles
to scatter fragments of pink flesh in tangents
burning outward through the air.
And from the bottom of the pool
the masked man swims upward
showing his teeth: black and shining gold.
In the dense, airless depths he suffocates.

In cold, peeling hallways, they take their pleasure.
It is an old tune, a hoarse and crackling voice.
Outside, the thick black smoke cracks into bitter smiles
of winter, and drops to the pavement in steamy
        fragments.
At night we squeeze the burning lovedrops from our
        skin,
and lie down. The new life stretches around us in all
        directions:
broken glass, shit, clogged needles, entrails gone bad,
as far as the eye can see.
Above the city, a pool of turbulent, fiery air
burns to clothe black, itchy flesh
in the luminous music of tropical lovedreams.
Pamphlets of the inner eye, mementos
of the heart's aborted yearnings.

From the bottom of the pool,
the masked man swims upward.
Sleek like a panther,
he pushes through the heavy, listless *eau des rêves*,
moving toward the dimmed, violent shower of sparks
burning at the top of the pool.

Saudade do Towbin

from Chicago, with whom I signed,
in September 1963, a suicide pact,
which he carried out.

In the dark cemetery chapel,
the mumbled Hebrew liturgy begins.
Father and mother stand, mute and listless,
their sweetest agonies hidden within
the dulled blank lines of a forgotten middle-age.
Below them their only son, whom they had
     abandoned,
glows in the casket, his arms clotted with old
     needle-marks.
It is the ring-wraith! The phosphorescent fire
of the dead soul in autumn. The candied leaves
     and flowers
of this cemetery lane glow with a wild,
     unrelenting light.
Deep in the womb, another forgotten son sleeps.

In the soiled streets of Chicago
the young blood runs freely,
in filthy, uncared-for El stations and alleyways,
running ever downwards toward an almost
     forgotten spring.
Who will be their mother when they sink
into the neon glow where madness waits?
I can do nothing, and turn back, moving blindly
through the lost snow of my dreams.

It is springtime now. The April rains beat against
my bedroom window. How I long to lie down
amidst the luminous cushion of flowers
which coat the rich, wet cemetery soil.

To My Long-Lost Relatives

These retirement capsules the drug companies
send to my shrink — so elegantly presented,
a little drama in themselves.
The image is all.
He is weak, his hand is heavy,
coming and going, ages within ages.
The hand trembles.
The watch falls to the floor,
its crystal broken.
Depressed, and chained to a dying
cardiovascular disease and thyroid disorders,
he stumbles across an icy field.

The wind sweeps shavings of birdsong
into my icy room.
In a Russian dream I see the grey flaky lips
of my own dead grandfather.
As the door shuts softly, the
gold watch, samovar, and recordings of Hebrew liturgy
fly off into a heavenly orbit.
They drop little flares: messages to us below.
"Everything's fine! The weather's great!"

It is always winter down here.
Even in summer.
The bubbles die on our lips.
Here too the fields are icy.

For L.H.

Her picture hides the woman.
The woman hides her pictures in a drawer.
The girl, frightened and breathless,
shields the woman's body-love: her baby.
All gentle, frightened creatures who swim
in your pale blue eyes,
swimming for love, for pity of love.

In a trenchcoat, wearing eye-shadow, you
      cross a dark avenue
slashed with orange streetlights —
for love, if we clasp it, fluttering near,
like a wayward butterfly.
From here, from there, from the next place —
the stations fly by. The place names fly past,
and the forest crowds around the train.
The crackle of starched, decorous diplomats
returns at night in the sleeping car
as you rummage in your dreams.

In the room, the child stirs
in the crib, whispering in a gauzy dream.
The father, far away, stiffens for a second
and then is released to slumber.
It is a secret.
The baby sleeps beneath
the pearl-handled dress sword.
Your gentle orchid eyes tell all: all the times,
the faces, the scenes.

As I sleep we stroll together,
through parks, long tunnels, and boulevards,
through colored winds, unfolding before us
      like gay petals.
In the park we shall waltz for love.
For love we shall go on waltzing.

Union Square

May Day, 1970

At this strange rally
of the lame, the halt, the aging,
the veterans of the Old Left file by:
immigrant couples, dressed in their best clothes,
marking the dignity of age and good causes.
Seattle. 1917. A faded photograph of Big Bill Haywood,
holding a sullen Siberian child.
At the rally, a tinny gramophone scrapes out the old
      songs.
The union, it says, is behind them.

And on a bench, near where I sit,
a soldier is making love to a girl.
He stupefies her with kisses,
turning and thrusting his tongue
deep into her mouth.

PART TWO

Warpoem to My Classmates

To rape, and then to quarter
the fragile human form.
Rustsearing bloodclotting stainless steel blade
cuts deep into my smooth and florid youth.

In the room, I sit among the beautiful ones.
Fragrant the poetry of their Yiddish eyes.
In the classroom I hold fast to them,
and think of war.

Alba, for a Strange Land

on writing to ask for a teaching post in Tanzania.

In the night,
I step out to mail a letter.
A chill wind is blowing,
here is the belly of the war-bloated dragon.
Across the world, in Tanzania,
the morning star of peoples' justice is rising.
Will they accept me?
I would ask the ancient Chinese
if this is an auspicious day —
of hopeful auguries for such an undertaking.
A German guard-dog growls in the darkness.
A great fear is abroad in this land.
The people are puzzled and angry.
Disgruntled, they run here and there,
seeking the causes of their pain,
never satisfied and growing always more confused.
The bloated dragon waxes ever more insane,
biting, in his rage, his own foul back-parts.

And in a far place, little known,
hope unfolds — simply, like the new green of spring,
or a gentle lady disrobing.
And the people breathe the air of a new day,
and are happy.

Winter in the Imperial City

Peking, 1971

Red guards scattered to the four winds;
all silent in the city of heavenly peace.
Pianist's hands, broken for Mozart, beginning to heal.
Farmers pass the smashed Buddhas — they will not
    mend.
Hot blood that ran in the streets, strong voices
    trembling to seize the future.
Ah, *mes semblables*! We thought it was the beginning
    of the world.
Pamphlets that raged against ancient walls —
a chill wind blows their scraps through the icy cabbage-
    fields.

To My Brother, Alan, at the Piano

The heart's forgotten rhythms — you repossess them.
Pure winds, ringing bells from a forgotten land,
shake the icy leaves outside our window.
When we were only boys,
you sought the holy sounds of secret places,
wandering in a joyous dream toward the center,
mixing sound and silence, laughter and heart's-pain.
Though we travel far from each other, meeting seldom,
I carry always with me your image:
fingers groping the silence, loosing magic sounds
to soar from the swirl-strings of your piano.

Three Yoruba Oriki

Note: These are three original oriki — *praise poems to the Yoruba gods* (orisha) *Eshu, Yemoja, and Ogun, who are worshipped in Nigeria, Cuba, Brazil, Puerto Rico, and even in New York City. Eshu is a trickster god, but more importantly he is the god of unforeseen catastrophe — the sudden eruption of human or natural violence that lays waste men's careful attempts to organize and structure reality. An* abiku *is a hypersensitive and sickly child, who often dies young and returns again to the same mother. Yemoja is the most profound of the* orisha, *and the mother of many of them. Dwelling in the ocean, she is wise, gentle, and very old. But Yemoja is also the patron of puberty, spring, and awakening sexuality. Ogun is the god of war and iron. A* favela *is a Brazilian shantytown; a* faziendero *is the owner of a large plantation.*

i. ESHU

Eshu makes nothing.
Stick your finger up the ass
of a mystery
and there he is — winking at you
from atop a skyscraper.
Eshu can fuck all night,
but he never conceived a child.
He torments the sages in their dreams.
And by day they wrack their brains,
seeking a salutary means of his disposal.

Flying on the wind — vicious they call him,
they who cannot understand. His passion
is a holy draught, pure his fire.
It is the live snake coiling and uncoiling
in the dark womb of happenstance.
Don't touch it! — you who count cowries
and shillings in the market.
Its froth the very mystery in our blood,
of underground streams transfused
with the pale phosphorescent glow
of magic rocks,
where ghostly fishes swim,
their eyes like monstrous lanterns.
There Eshu goes easily,
at home in the depths while up above
a solitary abiku child, wandering in the forest,
snuffs out, and laughter is heard,
gay but chill, thin in the halflit twilight.

Under the sun, that great bland stupid golden face,
you create and destroy, winding and unwinding
the sacred skein as it lays out its markings.
There, robed like Shiva in passionate forgetfulness,
you play out your violent game,
unmindful of the dull geometry of the lesser gods.

ii. YEMOJA

Waters of the dawn,
spirits illumined.
Sun rests — hovering.
Soft spindle, golden thread,
where bright fishes play at twilight.
A ring of pale green,
small shoots pushing up after the dry season.
Springing laughter where maidens bathe
in the morning rain,
new down on their shining thighs,
eyes bright with a wondrous knowledge:
thus it was in the beginning, new earth,
when the sons of God saw the daughters of men,
that they were fair.

In the darkest blue of deepest pools
you rest, and take your pleasure.
Goddess of the soft skin; aged mother looking on,
you have known all seasons
and blessed them — both the beginning and the end.
In secret places, you find your spirit's deepest calm.
Wrath of the torn waves,
ravager of a wild month, who can know you?
Mother of all, you cherish for your own
the girlchild's first moist and limpid kiss,
stolen by moonlight in the bush.

Cleansed by your gentle waters, Yemoja,
I bathe at the edge of the sea,
resting in a calm that is beyond me.
As I dream your great heart,
my tears fall among the waves
and go out to you on the stately flow of tide.
Princess and old queen-mother, you bless again and again
this foolish race of men, giving hope
with each returning spirit — each new blood
that flows, birth-bright, in the land.
All this, Yemoja, you hold and cherish:
these new beginnings on an old planet.

33

iii. OGUN

Outlaw. That you are.
First to come, first to go.
Across that river lies life.
Over those mountains is humanity.
On that hill is Prometheus the revolutionary.
He lies bound and gasping amidst an angry
      writhing favela.
Ogun goes first. Restless hunter, he prepares,
at the beginning, to drink the blood of births and
      endings.

Of gentility and decorum he knows little.
His is the bloody umbilical, the beads
of love-sweat on the laboring woman's brow.
His was the first hand to pick up the first gun.
Gu, god of iron, do not forsake us!
Change, a newness, revolution, beginnings again.
On the plantation Ogun is there
when the faziendero is stabbed a thousand times,
the bloated bursting hatred of centuries entering
his corpulent veins, while in another room his fair-
      skinned
mistress dies gasping on her rape-soiled sheets.
Who comes to drink the blood of heart and womb?
      It is Ogun.
When the people cry for justice, Ogun leads them
      in purity
to slaughter. When the white cock dies gasping
      and dancing
he comes to the red throat-slit, the magic orifice
of bloody shifting forces.

Ogun, you draw me back again when I would not go.
Justice raves in the streets — the simple justice of blood.
The dead live and walk again, crying for one last passion,
a final revolution. *Hasta la victoria siempre!*
In secret places, the passions gather. You call me to
them,
and I must go. In birth a woman's substance spatters
and stains
the earth. As her dark blood flows home, a child is born.
Ogun, because of you I know the blood's insistent
clamor.
At night I drink my woman's dark and bloodwet loins,
tasting the salt-lick and heart-throb there — and at dawn
I emerge to walk the grey and half-lit streets.
Revolutionary deity, celestial terrorist of the cutting arm,
you lead us to that gory place where the future will be
born.
And I follow you, now knowing why, craving to taste
the new thing you hold before me there.

1961270

Darkening Periscope

1914/1971

Something to say. Last words — of poetry.
Chill flowers bloom here.
Wind shakes the dry plants.
A dry fog floats outside the window.

A dream. You wake
from a torrid nightmare.
In a Fascist country someone is dead.
Beneath the bedclothes, you are smooth and warm.

Carlsbad; a lake. Laughing, clothed in a rich
        protection,
we stroll together. As you turn to the wind,
a dull perfume sweeps over you:
a drug from the mountains.

The promenade deck. This colonel is dying.
Clothed in suede and fur, we were never so envied.
All oceans — a mass of burning oil;
peacock's feathers startle the dead air.

Knight of wands. The young lie twitching in
        armchairs.
It is the wintery season.
At dusk the dead flowers flicker.
Aglow like fire-damp, they spit last flames in the
        still air.

A Dream of Lesbians

Stately; processional. They are children
of an Egyptian night

with their inward-looking eyes.
This journey lasts forever.

Adrift at the world's cool center,
my friends pass

in their paper boats,
masked in an underworld dream.

The boats glide by
without ripples.

It is like some single color, that spins away
as I try to grasp it — deep as the eye can see.

Passionate, indolent,
they are clothed in Egyptian black.

With calm blood, wide-eyed,
they drift with me toward morning.

A Walk in The Country: February

For M.L.R.

Blood on the snow.
It is the killing season.
These ash-grey woods are seething
with our ancient intimacies.
Like wayward birds, startled from their sleep,
the memories dance away from me,
flocking toward the forest.

The wind tugs
at my cape, my burning
frost-numbed face.
Some time long ago
I wrapped my arms around these trees,
enfolding them in boyish dreams
as I wandered through these fields.

Now it is winter.
In their scarlet jackets
the hunters scour
the black, ice-solid rocks.
Do you know, father —
I am holding still
to our old gay dreams, spoken by these woods.

Leaving Tangiers before a Storm

The sun
has turned away.

Wind shuffles
the curtains, idly exposing

the pale bellies
of palmleaves.

Heavy with luggage
we make our way toward the harbor,

past tourists with frightened eyes
and the vacant smiles of hustlers,

through dark and wind-blown streets,
shrill with the cries of children.

At noon the boat sets out,
from the end

of an overcast pier.
The sea is black and frothing,

and hustlers lounge on the quay.
Listless, with dark, empty eyes,

they watch us mount the gangplank,
and await the new arrivals.

My Blue Piano

*Translated, in collaboration with Miriam Frank,
from the German of Else Lasker-Schüler*

I have in my house a blue piano
On which I make no music.

It's been standing in the shadow of my cellar door
Ever since the world grew dark and savage.

Once four star-hands strayed across the keys.
— The moonwife sang in a boat —
Now dancing rats jangle the strings.

The keyboard is smashed. . . .
I mourn for this blue death.

Ah, dear angels,
I ate of bitter bread — and still survive.
Though it is forbidden,
Open the door of heaven to me.

I Arrived in That Town, Everyone Greeted Me and I Knew No One; When I Was Going to Read My Verses, the Devil, Hidden Behind a Tree, Called Out to Me Sarcastically, and Filled My Hands with Newspaper Clippings

Translated from the Catalan of J. V. Foix

What's the name of this town
with flowers on the steeple
and river with dark trees?
Where did I leave my keys?

Everyone says "Good morning!"
I go around half-dressed;
some people are kneeling,
another gives me his hand.

— What's my name? I ask him.
I look at my bare foot;
in the shadow of a barrel
a puddle of blood is shining.

The cowherd lends me a book,
I see myself in a window;
my beard has gotten long.
— What's become of my apron?

Such crowds there are in the square!
They must be waiting for me;
I, who read them verses;
they're laughing as they leave.

The bishop decorates me,
the musicians have already stopped;
I'd like to go home,
but I don't know the side-streets.

If a girl kissed me. . .
what would my job be then?
Now the doors close;
who knows where the pension is!

On a bit of newspaper
my portrait flutters;
the trees in the square
wave goodbye to me.

What do they say on the radio?
I'm cold, I'm scared, I'm hungry;
I'll buy him a watch:
what's his Saint's Day?

I'm going to Font Vella:
they've pulled up the benches;
now I see the Devil
who awaits me around the corner.

Paid Vacation

*Translated from the Catalan
of Pere Quart*

I've decided to go away forever,
Amen.

Tomorrow I'll come back
because I'm old
and have very sensitive feet
with swollen corns.

But I'll turn around the next day,
revived by disgust.
For ever more. Amen.

The day after that I'll come back,
like a messenger-dove,
as stupid as he is,
not nearly as honest,
or as white either.

Poisoned by myths,
with saddle-bags of blasphemies,
skinny and rebuffed, sleepy-eyed,
a prince naked down to his dream,
Job of the pigsty;
tongueless, castrated,
pasturage for lice.

I'll take the train of paid vacations.
Holding onto the edge.
The land which was our heritage
flies from me.
It's a stream between my legs
that rejects me.
Grass, piles of stones:
love's signs dissolving in shame.

Oh land without a heaven!

But look at me:
I've come back again.
All alone, almost blind from leprosy.

Tomorrow I'm leaving
—I'm not fooling this time —.
Yes, yes; I'm going on four paws
like a great-great-grandfather,
along smugglers' trails
right to death's black line.

Then I jump in the burning darkness
where everything is foreign.
Where the ancient god of our parents
lives in exile.

A Small War

Translated from the Catalan
of Gabriel Ferrater

They brought anti-tank mines, useless
and heavy as an historic symbol,
wrapped in capes soaked
with ancient smells, rosemary
and mule-sweat. And also German
machine-guns taken from fighter planes
and shells of English scrap-metal.
In groups of two or three, widely separated
from each other, lowly and stubborn
as termites in a great felled stump,
the maquis bored through the Pyrenees.
It was one of the smallest wars
we've known. I came upon
only one corpse. That of a young
peasant girl from Aragon, who climbed in
an army truck, and also made
an easy symbol. She amused
the driver and mechanic, and together the three of them
drove off a bridge. The girl
had a simple wound, nothing
interesting, but the doctors who did
the autopsy found a remarkable deformity
in her ankle, hereditary
in origin, drawn from far-off
roots in the racial tree.
And the pain of a moment, plus the pleasure
it brought, lost importance
before that millennial defect,
deaf and established. Nothing individual.
It was a war, though a small one.
And fantastically enough, there was
nothing personal in it either, the nausea
that seized me, an instant's protracted examination
and with the sun's help, which fiercely
punished the covered nook and coarse
threshing-floor with its stubble of crosses and bones
that was the hamlet's cemetery,

when the stench of death seemed
the smell of some filthy sex. Meaning
I was young like all those
who go to war, and the flesh
frightens them, and they mangle and abuse it.
All emblematic, immemorial.

At the Jazz Colón: Barcelona

The tallest
was the man,
refined, with long
fingers
and a blonde-haired wife
who danced with all the faggots —
even the queens. They loved it.
So did she, and her husband
pretended not to notice,
sipping his drink and watching
with a look of benign disgust.
One of our ships was in. The place
was jammed with angry sailors
looking for dope or an easy lay.
They danced with her
too. Everyone wanted
to dance with her.
The glamor of the rich,
a fairy tale
of beaches, fast cars,
the moon on the fragrant quicksand

while we sweated. Hot
September. Dancing
in the cramped and airless nightclub.
And the man, and the woman
were like royalty among us,
or the tired end of some boring
decadent novel.

To a Man Who Has Plucked a Flower

You look a bloody fool
holding that flower!
It's dead now, you know. It
doesn't live, only burns downward,
spinning, perhaps, through our torpid gravity
in its lax trajectory of silence.

But you wanted it! Didn't you?
Well, the "myth of ecstatic communion"
has got you now, holds you
with bonds of our human delirium, just as
Planck's "constant h" binds us in literal thrall.
We poets do not believe it.
Knowing better, and worse, we are
ravished again and again by our inconsolable
        isolation.

I want to touch without bruising
the inviolable center of things.
Asking questions, receiving punishments,
I am indeed like Oedipus. I am
like the man with the plucked, dying flower.

Near the Point of Production

Ah, that was a day!
The sky sat listless overhead.
The industrious clouds kept course.
I lay in that dazzling field,
nursing my smoke-filled cerebrum
and broken ankle.
Beneath the veil of skin
the dark blood gathered.

The way is long to the sun.
The air grows thinner.
The birdveins pop in secret
beneath the chlorophyl camouflage.
I myself was wounded.
Among the innocent surfaces,
the bright throbbing started.
In a cowfield in Vermont,
at a baseball game with Thoreau
as honorary umpire,
the blood-pools formed inside my foot,
and the cracked bones
shot spark-filled telegrams
to godhead.

The laser-cries of crickets
cram these woods.
It is the country.
The buzz-saws cut clean through,
shearing the air's smooth aspect.
The sun is a silver royalty,
globe without cross,
shimmering coinage of energy.
A monopoly of means,
of living, humming fluids.
And the eyes roam,
restless for change-of-state,
beneath the decorous leafy canopies.

Notes for a Lecture on Form

For G.S.

Form
I should say
is the soul's digestive system.
Or where you find it —
something new,
unheard-of.
I, myself, constantly
quaff such things.
All day long
I guzzle forms.
Agape,
I ogle sculpted traffic greenlights
and get an earful
of melodious garden treevoices,
or the metallic splash
of garbage-cans at 6 A.M.
All I see or hear is FORM.

The air inside my hat
is hat-shaped.
Leaflets fall from the air,
plunged to earth
and are reborn
in someone's accidental glance.
Or for my "cantos," at thirteen
I plucked pure Greek resonances
from my father's dual-dead-language dictionary,
grafting them onto
my adolescent glub
like wax wings.
They grew me then, now
seem so awkward.
And they were forms.
I walked on them like stilts,
like variable feet,
and I say now that
ALL THE SPIRIT CAN DIGEST

will fill my mind with voices
                              thoughts
                              music
                              historical tableaux
and the magic rattle of rainy days.

But then the water drum
is something else again.
Or the talking drum.
Again something else. Though
the taut umbilical is also like a drum,
stretched skin
through which the charged pulse
first flows freely.
And always I can hear the sound
of my own heart beating,
breath of my breath
flame of my fiery groin
rhythm of my dreams,
that which comes through the blood,
through the breath,
through the mouth sucking close,
and I'm still sucking, STILL HUMAN,
twenty-five years old and
I feel the pulse insisting
in myself,
in my human form,
my warm dream of life,
my celebrated "poetic device,"
the digestive tract
ruminative pamphlet
fiery eye
burst tympanum
all that the child's soul digests.
The darkest night, none darker,
cut by a crescent blade.
Or the baleful eyes of wolves
on children's bookjackets.
The greedy blissful-ignorant soul
of my own younger self,
devouring Pound and Whitman —
leonine starburst rhetoric.

And time,
that makes us make it new,
demanding of us death or life,
time — that surreal inquisitive,
unsent-for and unwelcomed,
insistent, paralyzing,
forcer of desperate stratagems.
In panic we make them,
our new forms. It is
like waking from a nightmare,
clasping a painful image
that fades ferociously to nothing
while we struggle to reclaim it.
Or the man on the handcar
his squeezed & sprung rhythms
lurching and pulling a relative time
truer than his mind's own eye.

AND IT IS INEXHAUSTIBLE,
fragrant, mindblowing —
what is, what is not,
what we devour absentmindedly for breakfast,
what I see in my handclasp
in my bloodrush
in my photographs and stopwatch.
This godliness
forced from the womb unspeakably
and WHAT THE SPIRIT CAN DIGEST
is not much, and reluctantly,
but necessary, inevitable,
for even the mind goes forward,
possessed by questions
by nightshade
by some horrible premonition
rushing toward which we leave our footprints,
accidentally,
where nothing was.

Bike-Riding by the Manhattan Docks

Bright spring day
and blaze of sunlight

lovingly
new-thawed

winds
caress me

I'm riding by myself
along piers

abandoned
to rats and cobwebs

gaudy intricacies
of Victorian industry

happy
my face warm

no one
just the waves

lapping
against old wood.

ABOUT THE AUTHOR

David H. Rosenthal was born in 1945 in New York
City. He has studied at the University of Chicago, New
York University, and the University of London. His
poems have appeared in such publications as *Poetry*
(Chicago), *The Nation* and *The New York Times.* He
has written about jazz and Latin music for *Downbeat*
in the United States and for *Jazz Journal* and *Jazz
Monthly* in Britain, where he lived for two years.
Assistant Poetry Editor of *The Humanist,* he has
contributed reviews and essays to *The Nation* and
currently lives and works in Barcelona. He is now
preparing several volumes of translation from
modern Catalan literature.